Looking at art

COLOURS

What colour is that?

national gallery of **australia**

Fiery hot, the strongest indeed
It can mean stop or danger
It's the colour of a big heart
You see it when you bleed

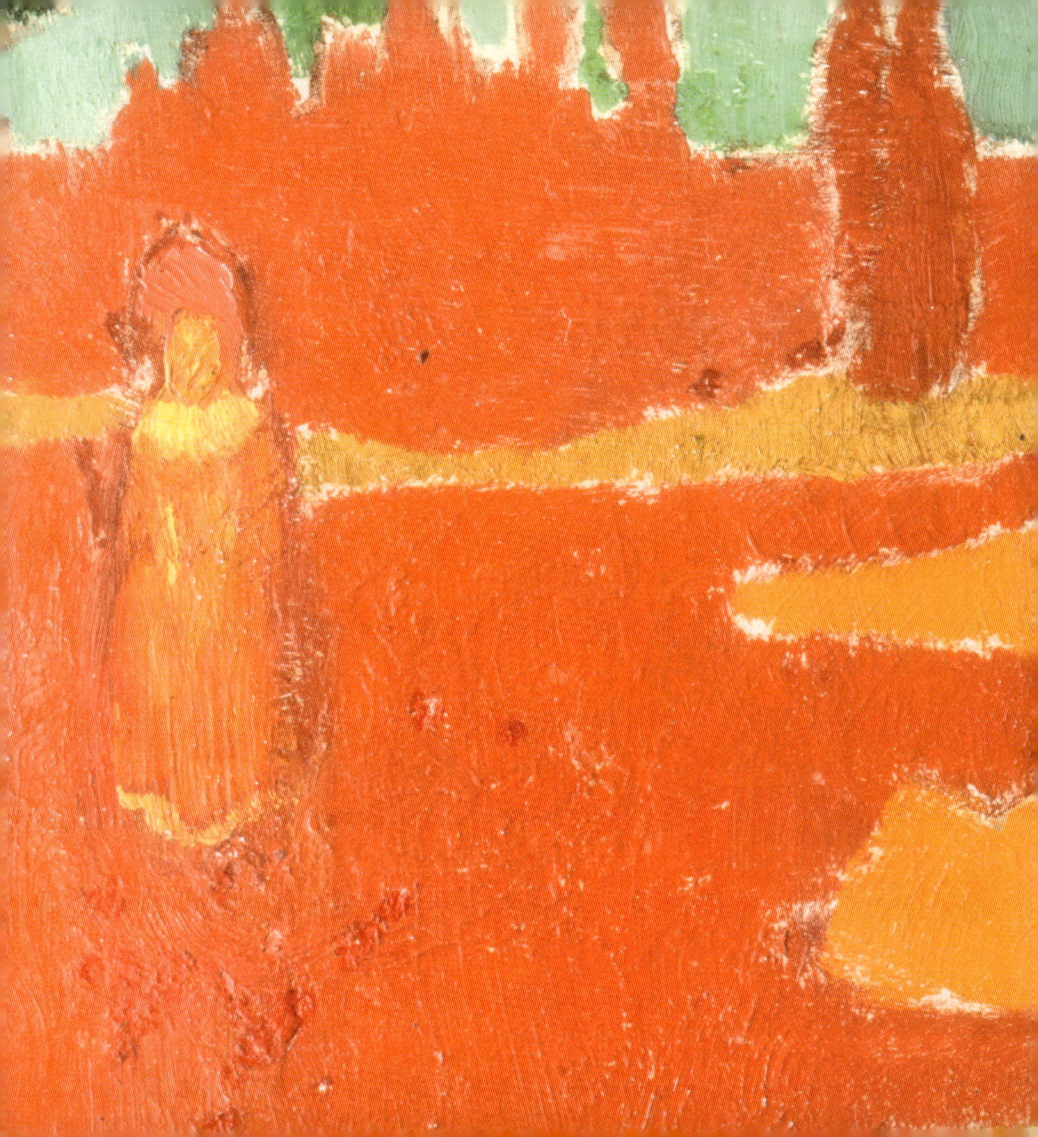

What colour is that?

red

It fills the sky
And oceans deep
It makes us calm
And ready for sleep

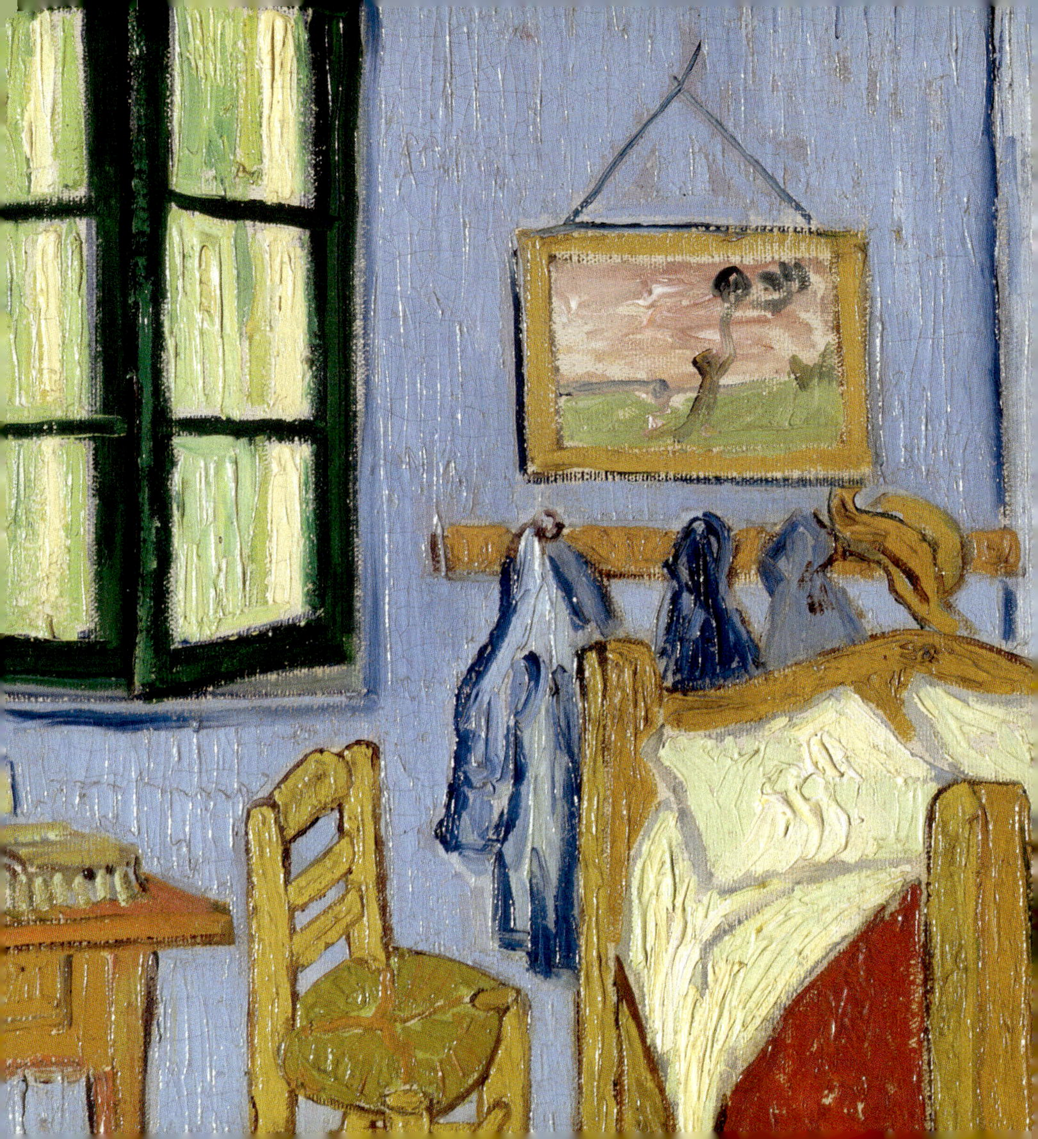

What colour is that?

blue

Light of a sunny day
Sand on a beach
Lines on a road
It's in our reach

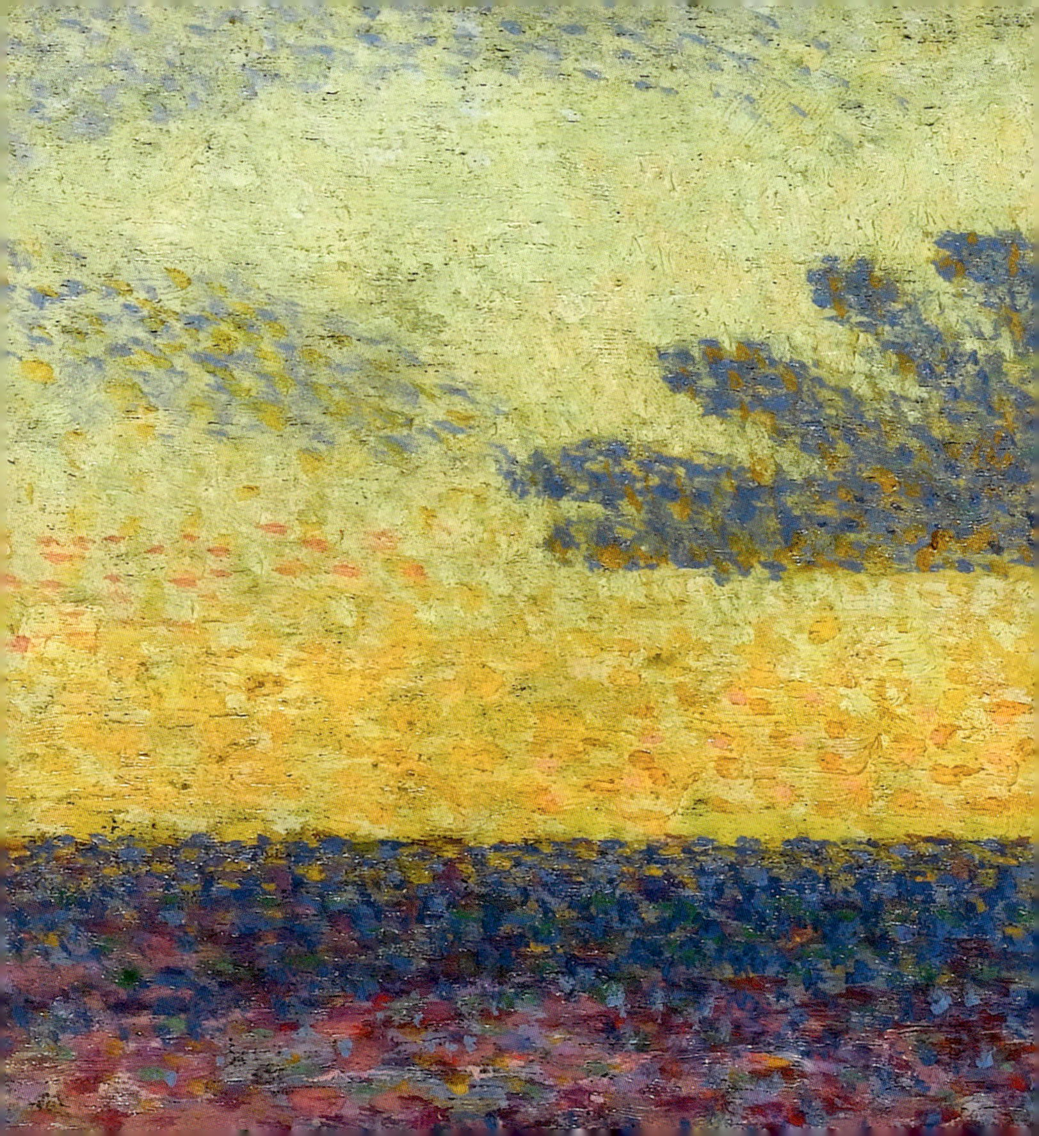

What colour is that?

yellow

Royal and regal
Serene and true
It appears on the palette
When you mix red with blue

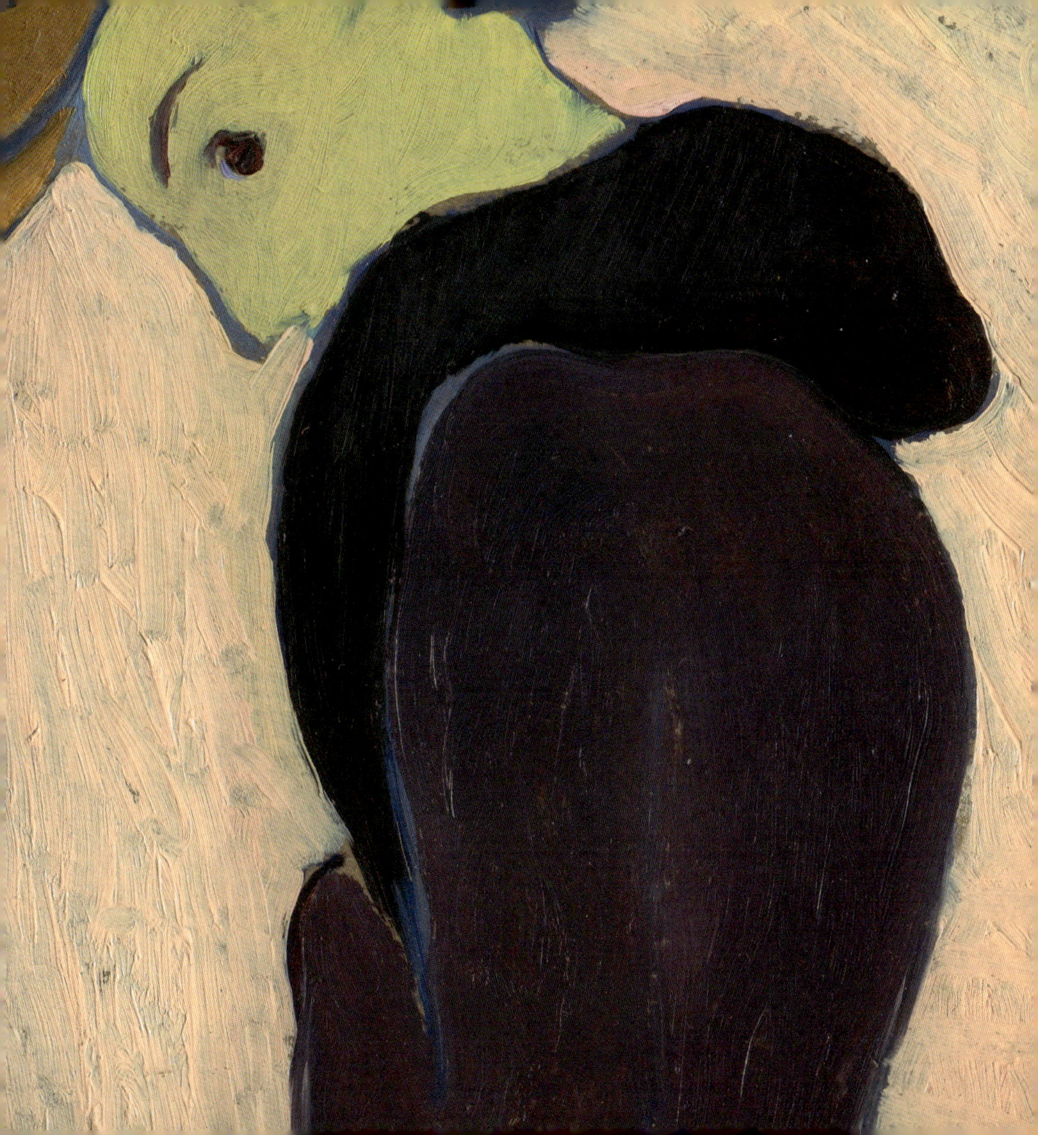

What colour is that?

purple

Flouncy and flamboyant
And fruity too
You can make it yourself
Mixing red and yellow

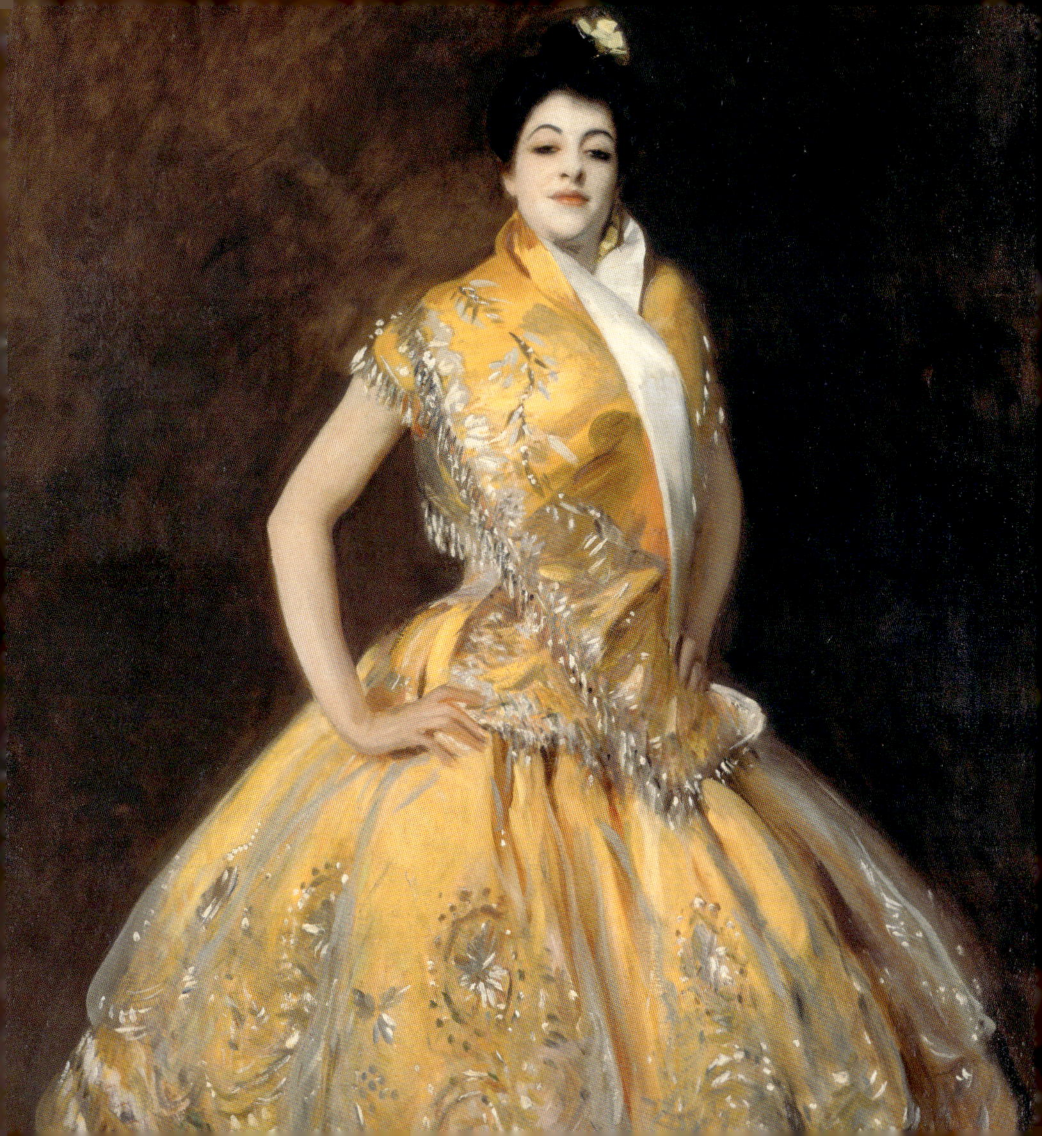

What colour is that?

orange

It's all around us
In the forest and the trees
It's not yellow and it's not blue
But put them together …

What colour is that?

green

Earthy, woody or dirty?
It comes from many colours
blue + orange
purple + yellow
green + red

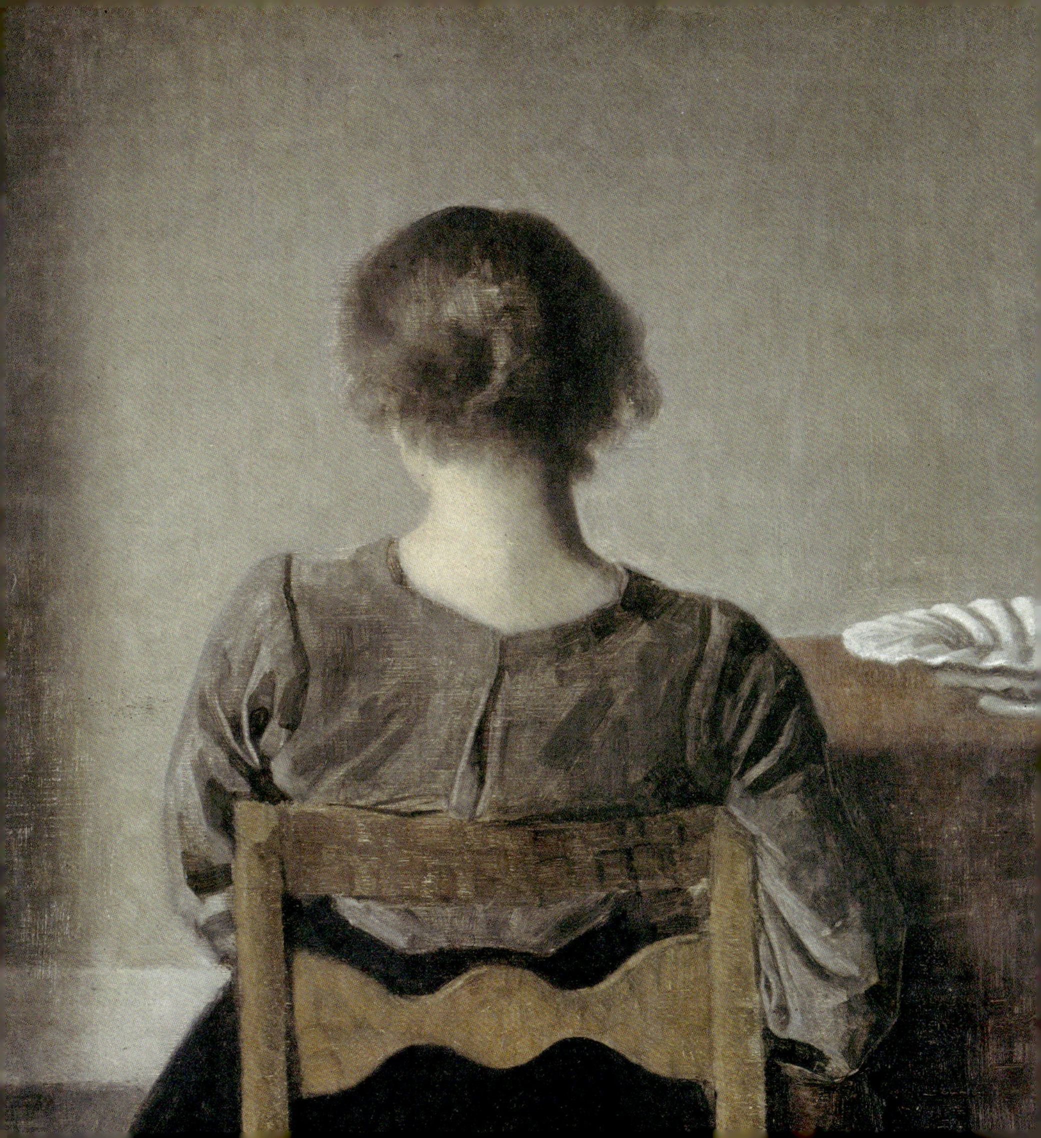

What colour is that?

brown

Bad or serious
Dark as night
It can make you sad
It's the opposite of white

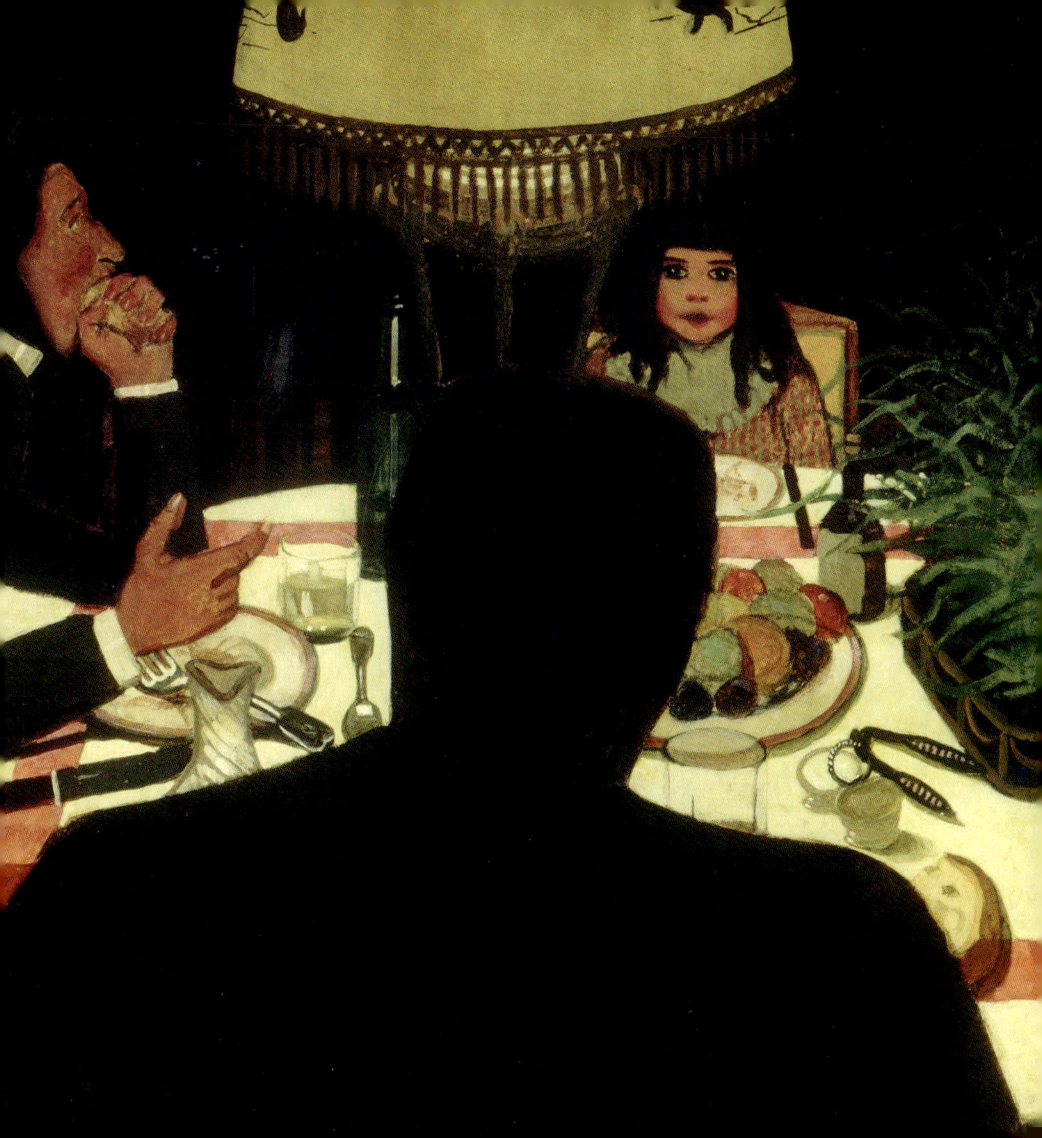

What colour is that?

black

It’s so light
You can see it in the dark
Like snow on a mountain
It glistens and sparks

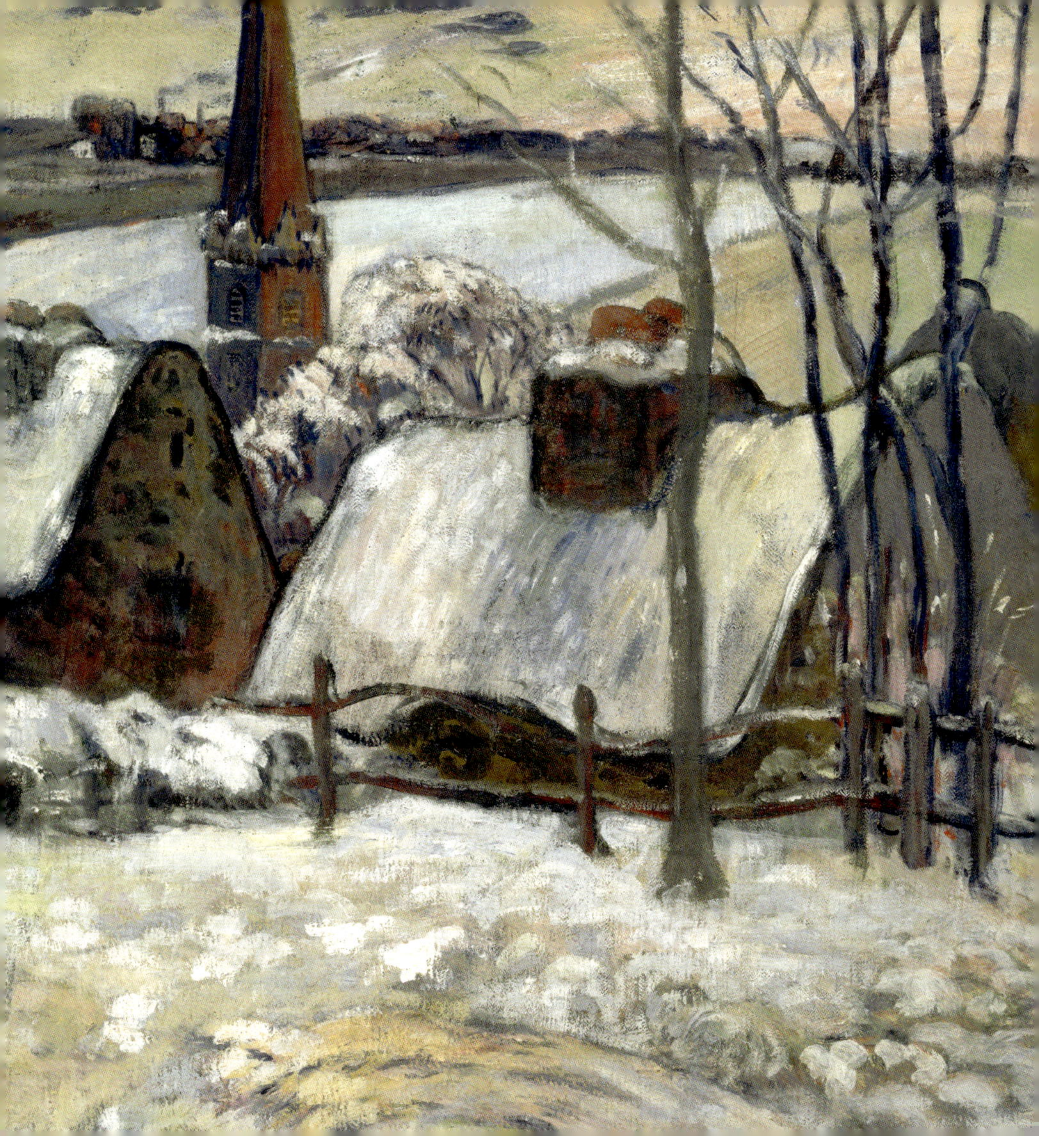

What colour is that?

white

Fairy floss and strawberry milk
It's pretty and it's sweet
A lovely colour to wear
And good enough to eat

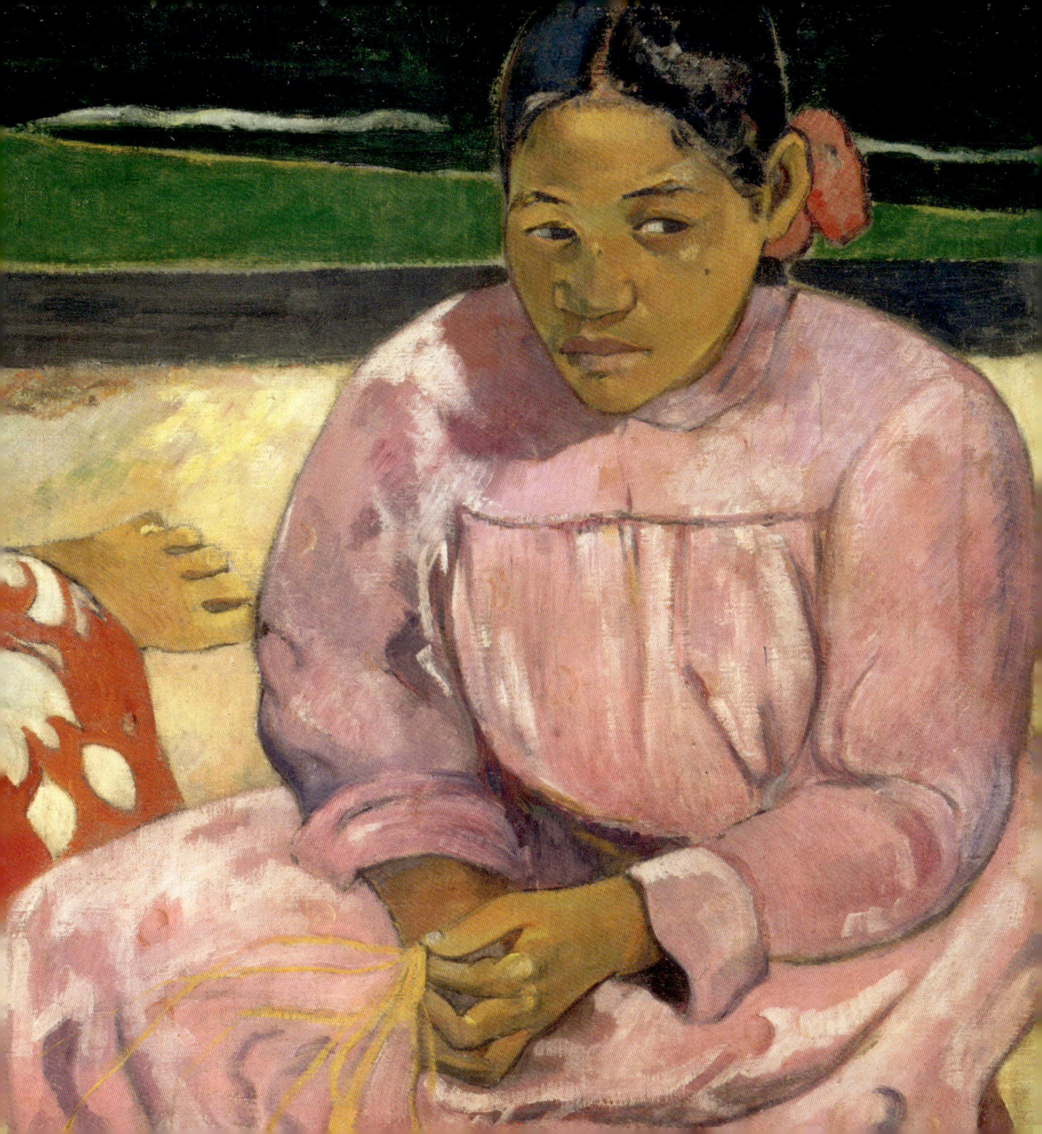

What colour is that?

pink

colour wheel

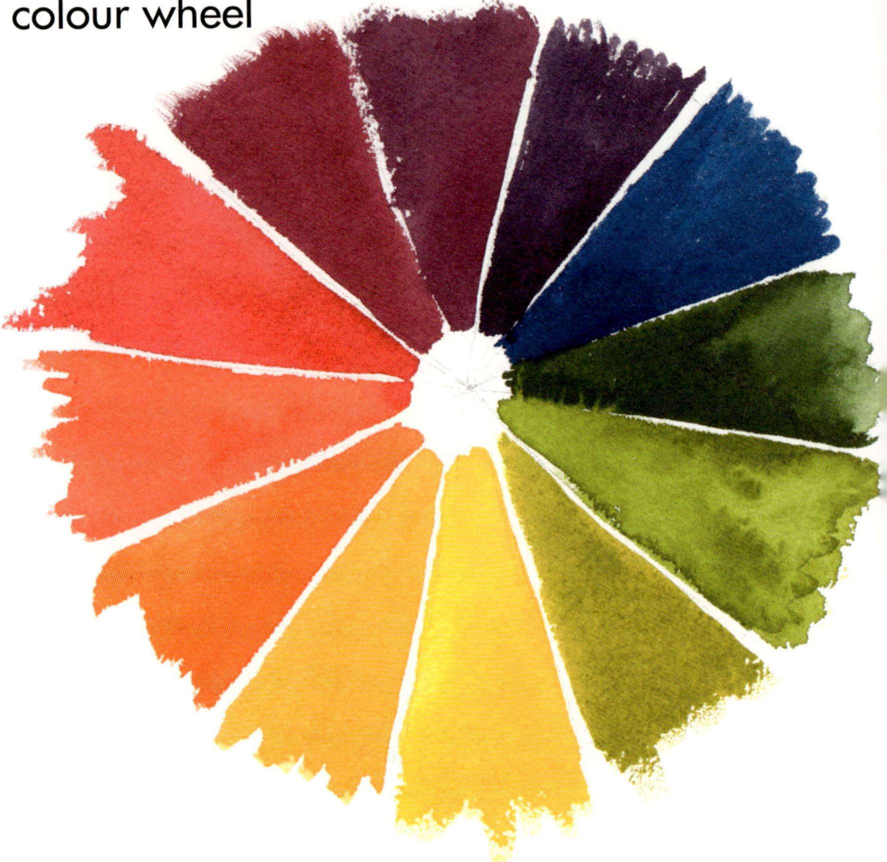

primary colours

red

blue

yellow

secondary colours

green

orange

purple

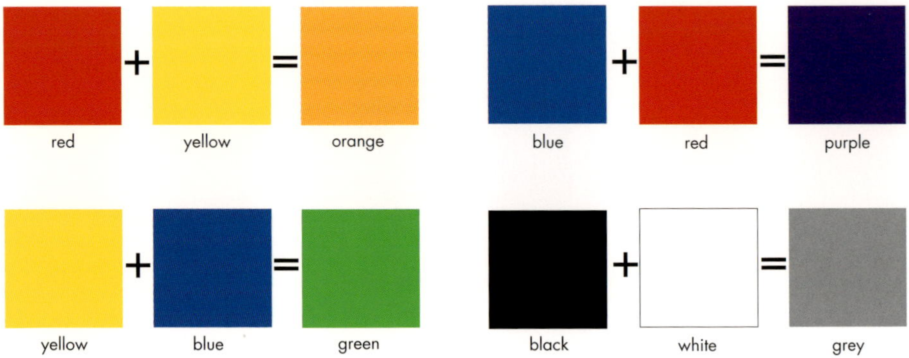

complementary colours

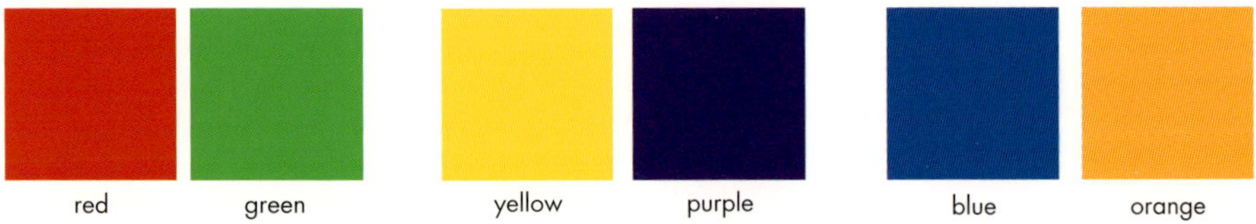

warm colours

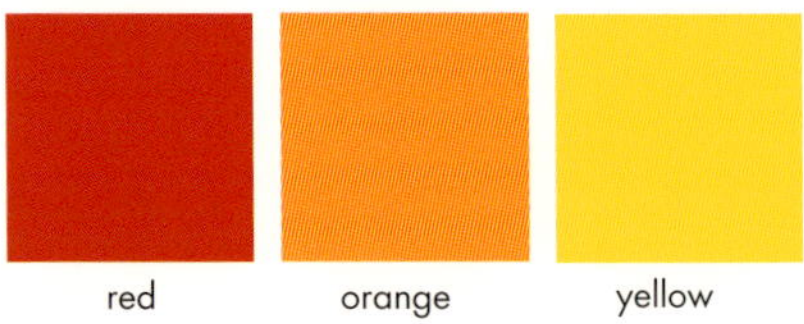

cool colours

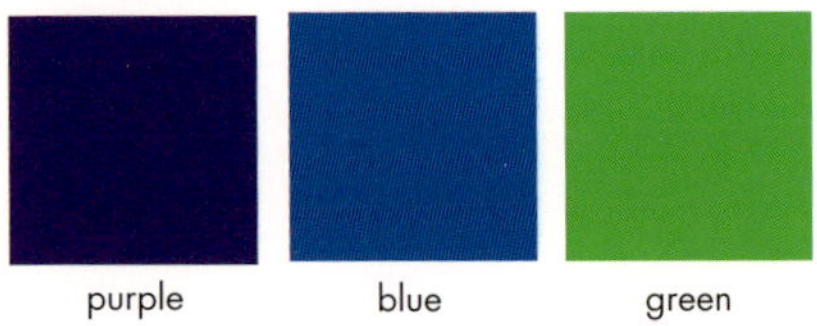

are the small squares different sizes?

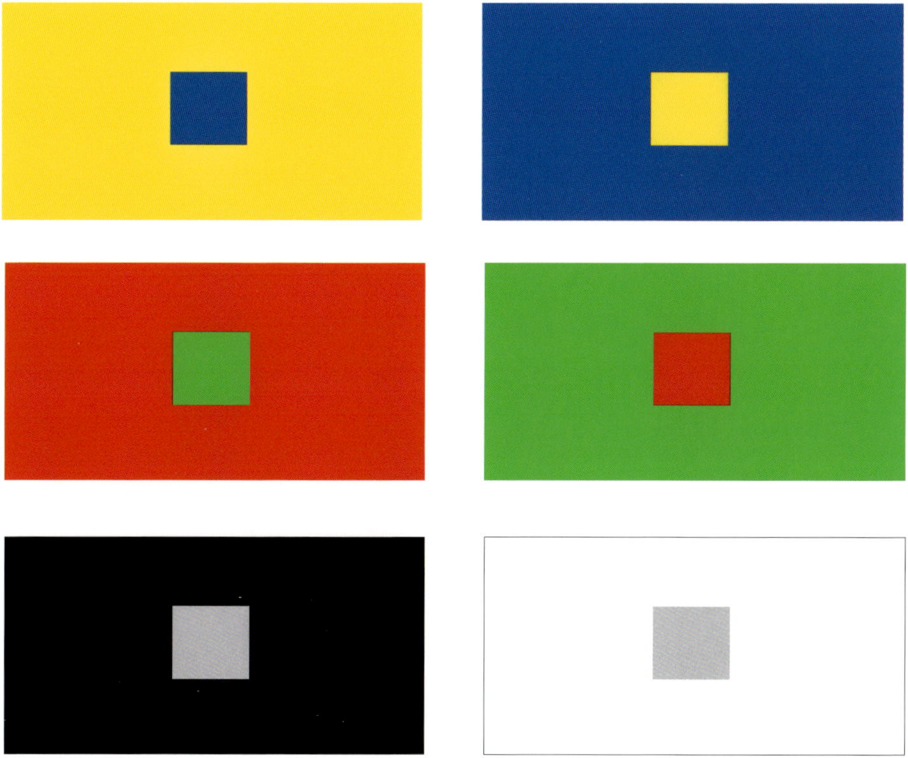

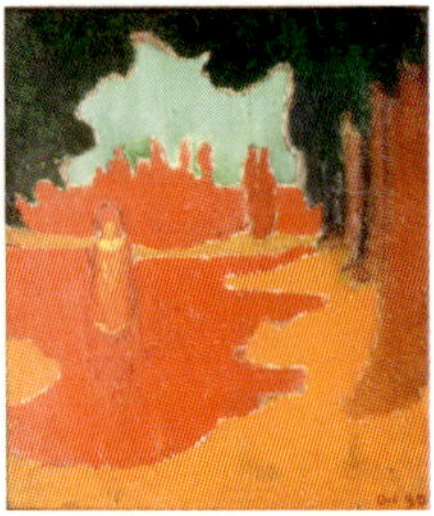

Maurice Denis
Sunlight on the terrace (*Taches de soleil sur la terrasse*) 1890
oil on card
24.0 x 20.5 cm
Musée d'Orsay, Paris, purchased 1986, RF 1986-70
© RMN (Musée d'Orsay) / Hervé Lewandowski
© Maurice Denis. ADAGP/Licensed by Viscopy, 2009

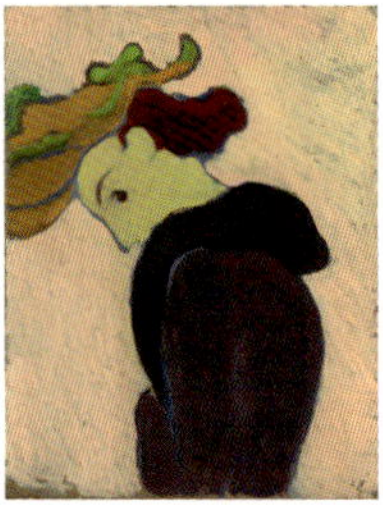

Edouard Vuillard
Profile of a woman in a green hat (*Femme de profil au chapeau vert*) c 1891
oil on card
21.0 x 16.0 cm
Musée d'Orsay, Paris, accepted in lieu of tax 1989, RF 1990-14
© RMN (Musée d'Orsay) / Hervé Lewandowski
© Edouard Vuillard. ADAGP/Licensed by Viscopy, 2009

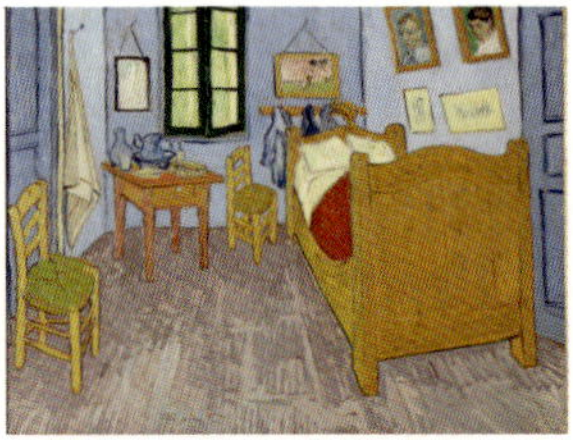

Vincent van Gogh
Van Gogh's bedroom at Arles (*La chambre de van Gogh à Arles*) 1889
oil on canvas
57.5 x 74.0 cm
Musée d'Orsay, Paris, transferred in application of the Peace Treaty with Japan 1959, RF 1959-2
© RMN (Musée d'Orsay) / Hervé Lewandowski

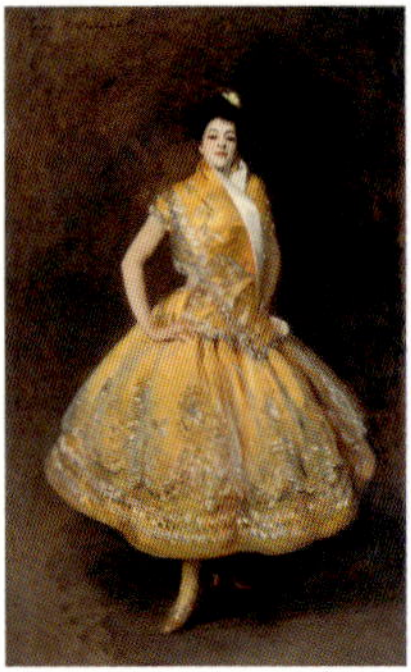

John Singer Sargent
La Carmencita c 1890
oil on canvas
232.0 x 142.0 cm
Musée d'Orsay, Paris, purchased from the artist 1892, RF 746
© RMN (Musée d'Orsay) / Gérard Blot

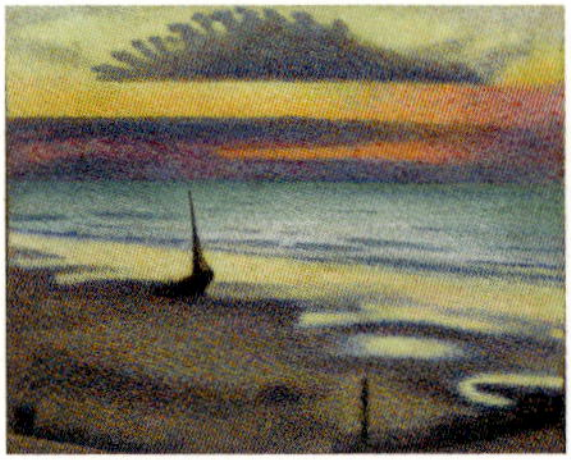

Georges Lemmen
Beach at Heist (*Plage à Heist*) 1891
oil on wood panel
37.5 x 45.7 cm
Musée d'Orsay, Paris, purchased 1987, RF 1987-35
© RMN (Musée d'Orsay) / Gérard Blot

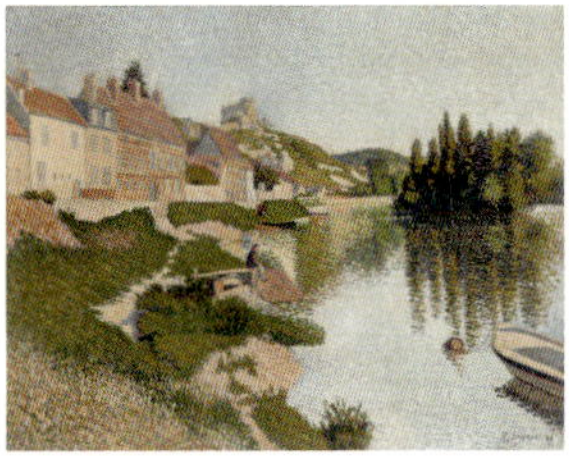

Paul Signac
Les Andelys (The riverbank) (*Les Andelys (La berge)*) 1886
oil on canvas
65.0 x 81.0 cm
Musée d'Orsay, Paris, accepted in lieu of tax 1996, RF 1996-6
© RMN (Musée d'Orsay) / Hervé Lewandowski

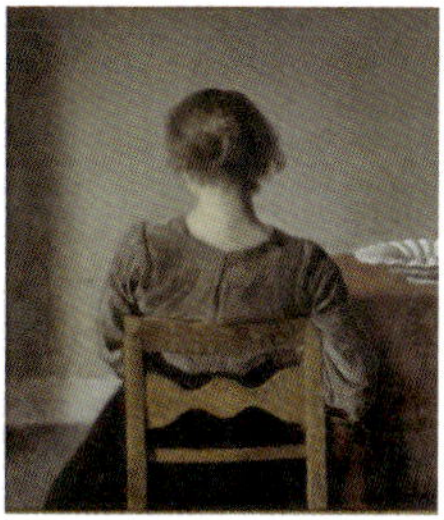

Vilhelm Hammershøi
Rest (*Hvile*) 1905
oil on canvas
49.5 x 46.5 cm
Musée d'Orsay, Paris, purchased with the assistance of Philippe Meyer 1996, RF 1996-12

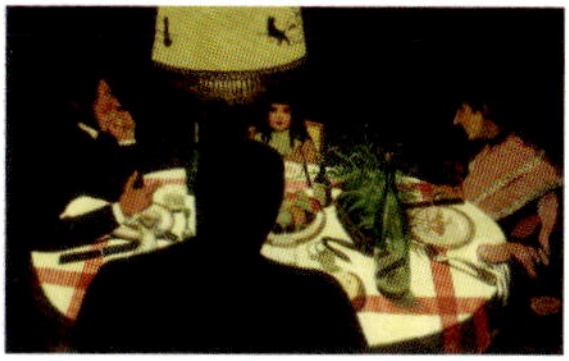

Félix Vallotton
Dinner, by lamplight (*Le diner, effet de lampe*) 1899
oil on card, laid on wood panel
57.0 x 89.5 cm
Musée d'Orsay, Paris, purchased 1947, RF 1977-349

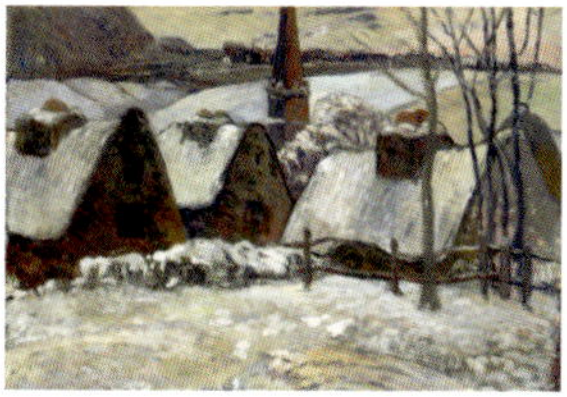

Paul Gauguin
Breton village in the snow (*Village breton sous la neige*) c 1894
oil on canvas
62.0 x 87.0 cm
Musée d'Orsay, Paris, purchased with funds from a Canadian anonymous gift 1952, RF 1952-29

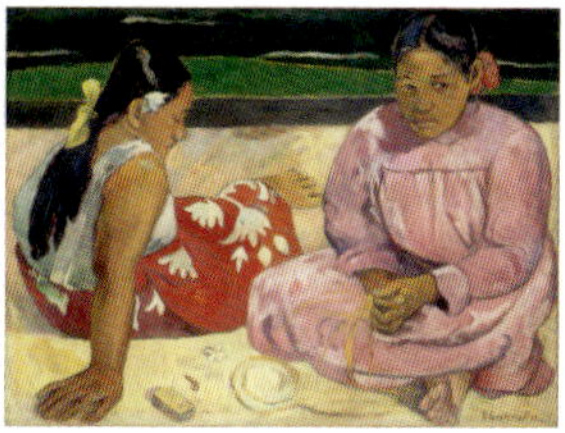

Paul Gauguin
Tahitian women (*Femmes de Tahiti*) 1891
oil on canvas
69.0 x 91.5 cm
Musée d'Orsay, Paris, gift of Countess Vitali in memory of her brother Viscount Guy de Cholet 1923, RF 2765

The National Gallery of Australia is an Australian Government Agency.

nga.gov.au

Produced by NGA Publishing,
National Gallery of Australia

Writing and development: Julie Donaldson*
Design and production: Kirsty Morrison*
Rights and permissions: Nick Nicholson*
Pre-press and printing: Blue Star Print (Vic)
* National Gallery of Australia

National Library of Australia
Cataloguing-in-Publication
Title: Colours. What colour is that?
Edition: 1st ed.
ISBN: 9780642334084 (hbk:2)
Series: Looking at art
Target audience: for pre-school age
Subjects: art appreciation–juvenile literature
Counting–juvenile literature
Other authors/contributors:
National Gallery of Australia
Dewey Number: 701.1

Published in conjunction with the exhibition
Masterpieces from Paris
Van Gogh, Gauguin, Cézanne and beyond
Post-Impressionism from the Musée d'Orsay
National Gallery of Australia, Canberra
4 December 2009 – 5 April 2010

Musée
d'Orsay

Distributed in Australia by
Thames and Hudson
11 Central Boulevard Business Park
Port Melbourne, Victoria, 3207

Distributed in the United Kingdom by
Thames and Hudson181A High Holborn
London WC1V 7QX, UK

Distributed in the United States of America by
University of Washington Press
1326 Fifth Avenue, Ste 555
Seattle, WA 98101-2604